DATE DUE	
APR 2 5 1996	
SEP 1 7 1996	
DEC 0 9 1996	
MAR 2 3 1997	
JAN 1 6 1998	
1-29	
2-12	
APR 1 3 1998	
27	
5-11	

DEMCO, INC. 38-2931

ANGEL FALLS

A SOUTH AMERICAN JOURNEY

Martin and Tanis Jordan

Kingfisher

NEW YORK

To Emily Louise Blamey

ILLUSTRATIONS: Scarlet macaws *above and endpapers*;
margay *front cover*; squirrel monkeys *back cover*.

The pictures in this book were painted on canvas using oils.

PRONUNCIATION GUIDE: The names of animals, plants, and places are
pronounced next to the name.

KINGFISHER
Larousse Kingfisher Chambers Inc.
95 Madison Avenue
New York, New York 10016

First American edition 1995
2 4 6 8 10 9 7 5 3 1

LIBRARY OF CONGRESS CATALOGING-IN-PUBLICATION DATA
Jordan, Tanis
Angel Falls/written by Tanis Jordan: illustrated by Martin Jordan.
—1st American ed.
p. cm.
1. Zoology—Venezuela—Angel Falls Region—Juvenile literature.
2. Natural History—Venezuela—Angel Falls Region—Juvenile literature.
3. Jordan, Tanis—Journeys—Venezuela—Angel Falls Region—Juvenile literature.
4. Jordan, Martin—Journeys—Venezuela—Angel Falls Region—Juvenile literature.
5. Angel Falls Region (Venezuela)—Description and travel—Juvenile literature. [1. Jungle
animals. 2. Zoology—Venezuela. 3. Venezuela—Description and travel. 4. Angel Falls
(Venezuela).]
I. Jordan, Tanis. Jordan, Martin, ill. [I. Title.
QL251. J67   1995
508.87 63—dc20   94–30243   CIP AC

ISBN 1–85697–541–X

Designed by Caroline Johnson
Printed in Hong Kong

At five o'clock in the morning we loaded our boat. In went supplies of dried food, pots and pans, a tent and sleeping bags, flashlights, matches, notebooks and pens, a camera, some spare clothes, and long curved knives called machetes ("ma *shet* ees"). By the time we had finished there was hardly any room for us. Scarlet macaws flew across the river as we pushed the boat away from the bank and set off.

We planned to travel up the Carrao ("Car *raow*") River to a mountain called Auyantepui ("Oye *ahn* te pwee"). Hidden in one of its canyons is the highest waterfall in the world, Angel Falls, "the river that falls from the clouds." In the wet season a fast boat could get there in a few days. But now it was the dry season, and in our small boat it would be a long trip with lots of time for exploring.

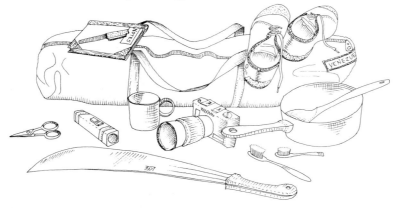

The wide Carrao River was the color of dark cherries, and in the distance a pinkish-gray cloud sat on the flat top of Auyantepui. At first the river flowed through the grassland, and this is where we saw our first big animal. A giant anteater carrying her cub shuffled across the stumpy grass and poked her long snout into rotting logs, looking for insects to eat. She found an ants' nest, raked it open with her great curved claws, and scooped up the prickly ants into her toothless mouth with her two-foot-long sticky tongue. As she shambled away, nosing for nests, seventeen side-necked turtles clambered out of the water to warm up, their solid shells shining in the sun.

In the rainy season the river floods into the jungle, and the current is strong. But even though this was the dry season, paddling upstream was still hard work. There were stretches of rapids where rocks and boulders

dammed the river, sending it rushing and gushing through the gaps and spilling over in small waterfalls.

At the first rapid we had to get out to pull and push the boat to the smoother water at the top. Purple flowers grew on the rocks, and their leaves trailed out under the water like slithery seaweed, so we kept slipping over. When we stopped to rest under a Guiana ("Ghee *ah* nah") palm tree, a herd of capybaras ("cap ee *bah* rahs") surfaced in the middle of the river and swam in a panic to the shore. Some scrambled onto an island and stood nervously among the bushes. Two others lurched onto the pebbly bank and barked in alarm. Then we saw why. Looking like an old log drifting with the current, came a caiman ("*cay*

man"), a South American alligator. Capybaras are the biggest rodents in the world, but in the river they have no defense against caimans.

Most days we started out early when it was cool and paddled until about half past three, when we would make camp. One afternoon we stopped under a cecropia ("si *croh* pee ah") tree. In the topmost branches two three-toed sloths munched on a fan of leaves. Tiny moths live in their long coats, safe from the beaks of birds. Sloths move so slowly that a plant called algae grows in the grooves of their hair and camouflages them from the powerful eyes of hunting eagles.

We were careful not to touch the tree, because biting azteca ("az *tay* cah") ants live in its hollow places. In return for a home, they protect

the tree. Should they sense the touch of a termite on its trunk or the soft step of a squirrel monkey on a branch, the ants swarm out and attack. Only the sloths are safe, protected by their thick coats.

Day by day as we paddled along, there was less grassland and more jungle, until eventually we left the grassland behind. At the top of a set of short, steep rapids, we stopped to examine our bruised shins. From the jungle came a thudding, drumming noise. Suddenly, with a great commotion, a herd of snorting, teeth-gnashing white-lipped peccaries ("*peck* ah rees") charged from the trees. Reaching the water's edge, the leaders saw us and stopped abruptly. But those behind could not stop. They tumbled over each other into the water, and swam to the other side. We counted more than a hundred peccaries scrambling up the bank and stampeding into the jungle.

A band of charging white-lipped peccaries, with their fearsome teeth and tusks, is a frightening thing. But a peccary on its own is vulnerable. An anaconda reared up from behind a log and coiled around the last peccary as it splashed out of the water. Each time the peccary breathed out, the snake squeezed tighter, until at last the peccary couldn't breathe in at all. Then the anaconda swallowed it whole. Now the snake wouldn't have to eat again for two months. Quickly we paddled on.

Daily now we drew nearer and nearer to Auyantepui. The river looped like a wriggling worm, and sometimes the mountain was on our left, then around a bend it would be on our right. During the day Auyantepui looked like a giant castle, pink and golden in the sunshine. But after sunset it could look like a dark and forbidding fortress, blue and slate in the gloom. Slowly we paddled, never knowing what we might find around the next bend, although we often traveled for days without seeing any large animals.

Finally we arrived at the Churún ("Choor *roon*") Canyon and the Churún River which would take us to Angel Falls. The Churún was very different from the wide Carrao River. In places it was narrow and fast as it frothed and splashed down fierce rapids, whisking whirlpools on its way. Between the rapids the water was deep and still. Small creeks were overhung with trailing vines and lianas ("lee *ah* nahs"). Large spiders with flat bodies and long thin legs sat flattened, barely visible, on tree trunks and scuttled out of sight as we brushed past.

Later than usual one afternoon, we paddled up a narrow creek past giant boulders, looking for somewhere to camp. The water was quiet and still, and as we drifted silently around a bend, we saw a family of four jaguars beside a rocky pool. Two of the cats were black, but the rosette patterns in their fur were clear.

The young jaguars were practicing their hunting skills, and their muscles rippled as they tried to scoop up the crimson and turquoise fish that shimmered in the shallows. When the jaguars saw us they slipped silently away into the shadows. Elated by the sight of such rare animals, we made a camp nearby, hoping to see them again.

We spent the next few days exploring the creek and the jungle. So that we would not get lost, we cut branches with our machetes to mark a trail. In places the jungle was so dense that we had to hack our way through.

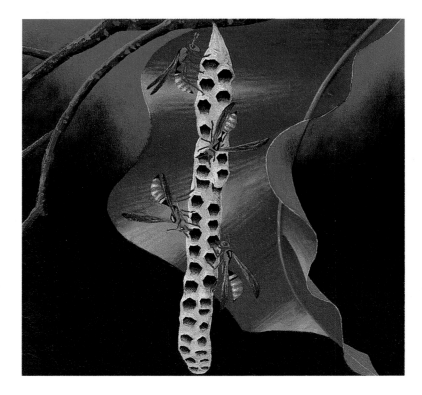

In a patch of sunlight a heliconia flower glowed gloriously crimson. Gliding down its dew-filled leaves was a coral snake. Some coral snakebites are deadly. Others are harmless. But even the venomous coral snakes are secretive and prefer to hide. Far more menacing was the long papery nest of stinging social wasps hanging from a twig. Warily we walked around them, marked the spot, and moved on.

Above us, with dazzling flashes of iridescent blue, two morpho butterflies fluttered by, then landed daintily on the fruity stem of a

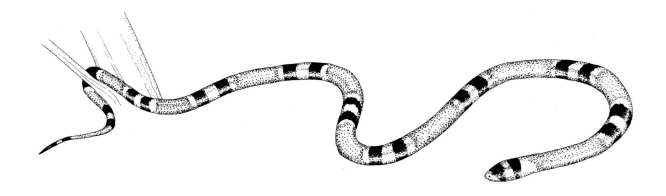

cashew nut. When their wings were shut the morphos looked like dead leaves.

From its hide in the cashew tree a bird-eating spider had come down to the forest floor to search for insects in the leaf litter. Nearby hovered a solitary hunting wasp. She intended to paralyze the spider with her sting and lay an egg on its stomach. When the egg hatched, the wasp larva would feed on the spider until it killed it. The spider scurried under a log. Patiently, the wasp waited.

On our jungle trails we had to move quietly if we wanted to see animals, but the jungle around us was seldom silent. Birds trilled and tooted, chortled and chimed, and whistled and warbled. "Haaaaaagh, haaaaaaaaagh," screeched families of scarlet macaws as they flew across the river to find food trees. "Hooo-whit, hooo-whit, hooo-whit-whee-oo," shrilled a screaming piha bird. Hornets hummed and horseflies buzzed. Peccaries trotted through the jungle braying noisily, and a tapir called its partner with a single, quavery whistling "whoooooo."

As we sat eating our cereal one morning, we heard a weird, eerie, wailing growl. The growling grew louder and louder, closer and closer, until it was a terrifying booming roar that filled the forest. The branches

of nearby trees began bouncing and shaking. Chunks of dead wood crashed to the ground, and suddenly a troop of red howler monkeys burst out onto the boughs above, defending their trees with deafening roars.

The quietest times were the hot afternoons, when scarlet macaws flapped silently home to roost. The jungle hushed, with only an occasional "oink," a sudden snort, or a raspy roar from resting monkeys.

At five o'clock came a whirring sound like a million buzz saws, as male cicadas vibrated the sides of their bodies to attract silent females. Then at sunset the jungle filled with a medley of noises: clicks and

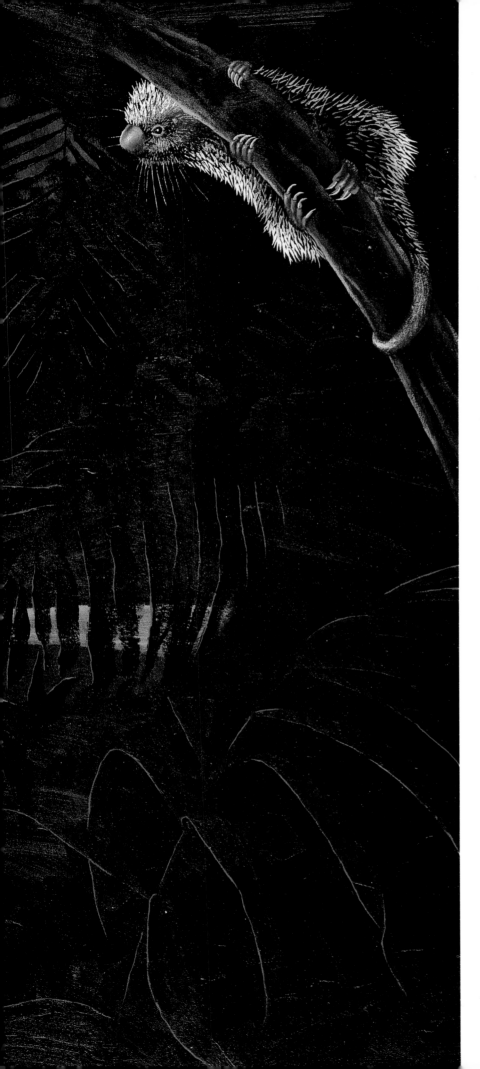

whistles from the tops of trees, screams and squeals from deep in the jungle, and sudden splashes from the river.

One evening, as our campfire blazed bright in the twilight and the scent of night flowers drifted on the breeze, a tree porcupine climbed onto a branch above the river and sniffed the air with its sensitive pink nose. Clinging tightly to a branch with its tail, it raised its quills and sat as rigid as a rock.

Prowling out of the jungle below were a pair of sleek cats. They were jaguarundis ("jag wah *run* dees") returning to their lair after a dusk-time hunt. But they were inquisitive and watched us for a long time before they padded along the riverbank to cross the river farther downstream.

In the moonlight the river was calm, smooth, and dark as molasses.
The shadowy jungle was filled with phosphorescent flashes from
fireflies, flying beetles whose twin green lights look like eyes.

"Peep-peep, peep-peep, whurp, whurp, whurp, rowuk-rowuk,
rowuk-rowuk, dink, dink, dink," chorused thousands of frogs and toads.
River frogs climbed out of the water onto rocks and logs, inflating the
balloons on their throats, to pipe persistently for partners.

Hearing them, frog-eating leaf-nosed bats, wings whooshing, took

off from a tree. They used the river as a path, the echo of their supersonic whistles and clicks bouncing off the water and trees to stop them from flying into things in the dark. The frogs couldn't hear the bats, but when they saw them they instantly stopped piping. The bats flew over their heads. Then the frogs began piping again, and the bats swiftly flew back to attack.

On a mold-covered boulder the marine toad croaked all the time. It knew the bats wouldn't bother it because it was so poisonous.

The craggy cliffs of Auyantepui towered around us as we continued up the Churún. The river became rockier and rockier. At night we were woken by the thunderous rumble of great boulders toppling from the cliffs and crashing down into the canyon. In time the jungle would grow over them.

One afternoon as we collected firewood we heard an armadillo rooting and rummaging in the leaf litter, gobbling up grubs. Under a spiny palm tree it stopped and began to dig, holding its breath so dust wouldn't go up its nose. Creeping up on the armadillo was a small spotted cat called a margay. Alarmed, the armadillo flattened itself on the ground, tucking its legs under its armored back. The margay tried to turn it over, and without warning the armadillo sprang three feet into the air. The margay hadn't expected this and swiped at the armadillo, but missed. Landing on its feet near one of its burrows, the armadillo zigzagged across the ground and bolted inside to safety.

Between the churning amber water of the rapids were calm stretches and shaded pools where the deeper water looked black. Often the water's surface was littered with dead leaves, twigs, and dust, and paddling across was like sliding over a dusty mirror. Our boat swept away the dust like a broom, making the water shiny again. Perched on a passion vine, a ringed kingfisher watched for fish disturbed by our paddles. A dragonfly skimmed across the surface of the water and laid her eggs on a leaf. Pygmy kingfishers like jet-propelled jewels darted out to catch insects.

As we were making coffee one morning, two king vultures soared through the sky and hovered to a halt on a dead tree beside our camp. They spread their wings for the early morning sunshine to warm their feather oils, and as they jostled each other for space, they became angry and their heads became redder and redder.

When we set off, the sky was peachy with sunlight. It seemed it would be another hot, cloudless day, and as we traveled along we kept jumping in the river to cool down. But later that afternoon the weather changed dramatically. The sky turned an ominous yellowish-gray. The jungle became quiet and still. From above the mountain came a deep grumbly rumbling, followed by the crackety-crack-crack of thunder.

Across the canyon, a barred forest falcon rested in a kapok tree. It had caught a tree snake to take back to its young. A green iguana basked on a branch nearby. From the tip of his scaly nose to the end of his slender tail he was six feet long. Tiny, biting black flies attacked our ankles, and we hurried to make camp.

That night the wind whooshed through the jungle, billowing and lashing the tent. Just when we thought we would be blown away, it began to rain so heavily and loudly that we couldn't hear each other speak. It rained for days. The wood was too wet to make a campfire, and everything was cold and moldy. Our skin was clammy, and we felt as if we were turning into frogs.

At last, the rain stopped. The sun came out and the jungle steamed. But on top of Auyantepui it was still raining.

The river had risen ten feet, and the water surged past our camp in a
swirling muddy torrent. We hung our soggy clothes on bushes to dry.
It was too dangerous to travel, so we spent the days looking for
wildlife. One morning, while walking in the jungle, we glimpsed flashes
of bright color. Deep in a thicket of vines and lianas, fourteen flame-
orange male cock-of-the-rock birds were waiting for three brown
females to settle in the branches above. Then, one after another, the
male birds flew down to display. Each one spun in a circle, then sat
silent and still, flaunting its fiery feathers on the forest floor.

After three days the river level dropped, the fast flow slowed, and we set off again. Late that afternoon we came to where a narrow river, full of fallen trees, surged into the Churún. It was the Angel River.

The next morning, with the valley full of steamy dawn mist, we set off to walk to the base of the falls. Auyantepui was wrapped in clouds, and the metallic call—"tink, tink, tink"—of a bearded bellbird echoed through the canyon. It had rained in the night, and as we scrambled up over boulders, the dripping jungle smelled of wet earth and damp leaves. In the trees above, a troop of squirrel monkeys twittered crossly at us.

We stopped to rest in a clearing where an enormous tree had fallen. Through the gap where the tree had once stood we saw the clouds begin to rise above the cliff. The mist melted away, and there in front of us was Angel Falls, the highest waterfall in the world. As if in slow motion, the water poured and tumbled for half a mile, hitting the boulder-strewn valley below in a vast veil of vapor that formed the Angel River.

The jungle seemed still; even the monkeys were quiet. Then, on the wind, we heard the roaring of the water. A faint spray touched our faces from "the river that falls from the clouds."

GLOSSARY OF ANIMALS IN THIS BOOK

SCARLET MACAW—*Bird, endpapers*
Three feet long from head to tip of tail feather. Scarlet macaws fly by day and are vegetarians, eating fruit, seeds, nuts, and leaves. They nest in holes in trees. With their tough beaks they can crunch up nut shells and gnaw at rocks to find salt.

GIANT ANTEATER—*Mammal, page 9*
Six feet long, though a lot of this length is tail. Giant anteaters are insectivores and need to eat more than thirty thousand insects every day. Because they can't retract their claws, giant anteaters walk on their knuckles.

CAPYBARA—*Mammal, page 10*
The largest living rodents in the world, capybaras can weigh up to 140 pounds. Capybaras are herbivores; they eat grass, leaves, water plants, and the bark of certain trees. Capybaras have slightly webbed feet and are excellent swimmers. They can stay under water for up to five minutes.

THREE-TOED SLOTH—*Mammal, page 11*
Sloths can't see or hear very well. Some sloths stay in the same tree all their lives and some sleep for eighteen hours a day. Their hair parts down the front and falls toward the back so that when they hang beneath a branch, the rain runs off.

GREEN ANACONDA—*Reptile, page 14*
Anacondas are the biggest snakes in the world and can grow more than 30 feet in length. They eat peccaries, deer and other mammals, caimans, and fish. Anacondas can stay submerged for ten minutes. They give birth to live young.

SOCIAL WASP—*Insect, page 18*
Social wasps build a paper nest from wood that they chew up. They raise their young in little chambers in the nest, which is suspended under broad leaves to keep dry. If disturbed they swarm out ready to sting.

BIRD-EATING SPIDER—*Spider, page 19*
South American bird-eating spiders are the biggest in the world. Although they have been known to eat newly hatched birds from the nest, they mostly eat large insects, frogs, and toads. If attacked, a bird-eating spider can scrape off some of its poisonous hairs and cloud the air so the attacker breathes them in. They also have a venomous bite.

CORAL SNAKE—*Reptile, pages 4 & 18*
Three feet long with a venomous bite. Brightly colored snakes are often venomous, and predators leave them alone. Other snakes look like coral snakes and they too are left alone even though they are not venomous. Coral snakes are carnivores; they eat other snakes, birds, frogs, and insects.

SIDE-NECKED TURTLE—*Reptile, page 8*
Most turtles protect themselves by pulling their heads into their shells but side-necked turtles lay their heads along their shoulders outside their shells. Turtles are omnivores; they eat insects, fruit, fish, and leaves.

CAIMAN—*Reptile, page 10*
Caimans are South American alligators. Cold-blooded, they control their temperature by basking in the sunshine. In the cooler night air they submerge in the warmer river water, keeping the tip of their snouts out of the water.

WHITE-LIPPED PECCARY—*Mammal, page 12*
Peccaries are omnivores; they eat leaves, roots, reptiles, birds, and mammals. Peccaries can be aggressive. Sometimes, one peccary will confront a predator and the rest of the band will rush to its rescue.

JAGUAR—*Mammal, page 16*
The jaguar is the biggest cat in South America, with a body more than six feet in length. It is the only big cat that doesn't roar and the only one that kills by biting through the skull. Of the world's big cats only the lion and the tiger are bigger.

HUNTING WASP—*Insect, page 19*
Hunting wasps are solitary and prefer to nest alone. Some species of hunting wasps sting spiders, then dig a hole and bury them. They lay an egg on the spider, and when the larva hatches it eats the spider and digs its way out.

MORPHO BUTTERFLY—*Insect, page 18*
Some of the biggest and most brilliant butterflies in South America, adult morpho butterflies feed on tree sap and over-ripe fruit. North America has 763 species of butterflies, but Venezuela alone has thousands of species. No one knows how many species there are in the whole of South America.

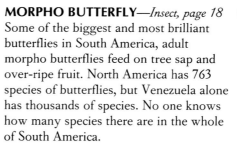

HOWLER MONKEY—*Mammal, page 21*
These are the noisiest animals in the world. Their roars can be heard more than a mile away. Howler monkeys are omnivores; they eat leaves, nuts, fruit, lizards, and birds.

TREE PORCUPINE—*Mammal, page 23*
The tree porcupine is a rodent that eats fruit and cracks nuts with its powerful teeth. It erects its sharp spines in defense when threatened, and can grip branches with its tail.

MARINE TOAD—*Amphibian, page 25*
Marine toads eat insects. Their bite is not venomous but they produce poison from glands in the back of their necks and so they are left alone by most predators. Adult marine toads can weigh more than two pounds.

FROG-EATING BAT—*Mammal, page 24*
There are more than two hundred species of bats in Venezuela alone. The frog-eating bat has a wingspan of 4 inches but some bats have a wingspan of over six feet. Bats are the only flying mammals.

NINE-BANDED ARMADILLO—
Mammal, page 26
Armadillos are the only mammals protected by a shell. They always give birth to quadruplets, all male or all female. When frightened or stressed, they can spring up like a jack-in-the-box; this is called "pronging."

KING VULTURE—*Bird, page 29*
The king vultures have very powerful beaks and a wingspan of over six feet. Vultures eat dead animals, but king vultures have a poor sense of smell and so they fly up high, watching where other vultures are collecting. Then they fly down, chasing smaller vultures away.

BARRED FOREST FALCON—*Bird, page 30*
Falcons are birds of prey, like eagles and hawks. The barred forest falcon is about 12 inches high. Its special prey is ant-birds that feed on army ants. It also hunts other birds, small mammals, reptiles and insects.

BEARDED BELLBIRD—*Bird, page 33*
The bearded bellbird is 10 inches high and has a bundle of beardlike loose skin dangling from its throat. Three thousand of the world's 9,000 species of birds live in South America, but less than 700 species live in the whole of North America.

JAGUARUNDI—*Mammal, page 22*
Jaguarundis are up to four feet in length and are active at dusk and dawn. Jaguarundi means "jaguar of the water." They are good swimmers, and always live near water. Jaguarundis are omnivores; they eat small mammals, birds, frogs, fish, lizards, and fruit.

FIREFLY—*Insect, page 24*
Night-flying beetles up to 1½ inches in length. They can flash twin green lights on their backs that look like eyes. There are many species of fireflies and some can light up their abdomens as well.

FROGS—*Amphibians, page 24*
In the South American jungle frogs live everywhere, from the river bank to the tops of trees. They vary in size from half an inch to five inches in length. New species of frogs are still being discovered in South America.

MARGAY—*Mammal, page 26*
One of the smallest South American cats with a body length of up to 30 inches. A margay hunts small mammals, birds, lizards, and frogs. It spends most of its time in the trees.

KINGFISHERS—*Birds, page 28*
Brightly colored kingfishers with long sharp beaks nest along the riverbank. They are active all day catching fish and flying insects. The pygmy kingfisher is 6 inches high and is the smallest species in South America.

TREE IGUANA—*Reptile, page 30*
Tree iguanas are more than six feet long. They are cold-blooded and climb to the tops of trees to get the early morning sun. When threatened, iguanas erect their neck spines and lash out with their tails.

COCK-OF-THE-ROCK—*Bird, page 32*
Adult birds are 12 inches high. They feed on fruits. The male is vivid orange and has a circular crest of feathers on top of its head. The female is brown. They are from the Cotinga family of which there are 90 species in South America.

SQUIRREL MONKEY—*Mammal, page 34*
Up to 30 inches in length including a tail of up to 17 inches. The squirrel monkey can't hold on with its tail, which is used for balance. Like the anteater, they wrap their tails around their shoulders for warmth at night.